CRASH COURSE

— on —

Jesus

ΟΥΚΓΑϹΠΕΔΟΝ ΛΛΟ
ΜΑΤΙΟΥΛΑΥΤΟΥΚΑΙ ΟΥΤΟΕΓΧΟΝ
ΟΙΗ✝ΑΝΤΟΔΙΕϹΩΘ ΤΟϹΤΟ
ΑΝ ΤΟΤΕΠΡΟϹΕΡΧ ΑΝ
ΛΙΤΩΙΫΑΠΟΙΕΡΟϹΟΛΥ ΠΟ
ΩΝΦΑΡΕΙϹΑΙΟΙΚΑΙ
ΑΜΜΑΤΕΙϹΛΕΓΟΝΤ
ΑΤΙΟΙΜΑΘΗΤΑ
ΑΡΑΒΑΙΝΟΥϹΙΝ
ΑΡΑΔΟϹΙΝΤ
ΠΕΡΩΝΟΥ
ΤΑϹΧΕΙΡΑ
ΗΕϹΘΙΩ
ΟΚΡΙΘΕΙ
ΑΤΙΚ
ΙΝΕ
ΝΟΥ
ΕΝ

CRASH COURSE

— on —

Jesus

SIX SESSIONS

CHRISTIANITYTODAY
INTERNATIONAL

BIBLE STUDY

Standard®
PUBLISHING
Bringing The Word to Life

www.standardpub.com

Published by Standard Publishing, Cincinnati, Ohio

www.standardpub.com

Copyright © 2008 by Christianity Today International

Editor: Brad Lewis

Creative Development Editors: Kelli B. Trujillo and Roxanne Wieman

Contributing Authors: Bill Barton, Lee Eclov, Steve May, Mark Mitchell, Leon Morris, JoHannah Reardon, Kristi Rector, John Guest, and the *Big Idea Discussion Guide*

Cover and interior design: The DesignWorks Group

ISBN 978-0-7847-2248-0

14 13 12 11 10 09 08   9 8 7 6 5 4 3 2 1

CONTENTS

How to Use This Study in Your Group

As Christians, we are a people of the Book. We base most of our knowledge of God and our faith in God on what we read in the Bible. It's critically important that we continually take up our Bibles and pursue a greater understanding of the text and the God who is revealed through it. The goal of the Crash Course Bible Studies series is to help you and your group become more comfortable, knowledgeable, and interested in the Bible—to aid you in that great pursuit of discovering God through his written revelation.

So whether you're a brand-new Christian or a seasoned believer, whether you've read from the Bible every day of your life or are just cracking it open for the first time, you'll find in Crash Course new insights, fresh challenges, and material to facilitate dialogue.

JESUS

In this Crash Course Bible study, you'll follow the story of Christianity's central character: Jesus Christ, the Son of God. Jesus of Nazareth was no ordinary man. His birth, life, death, and resurrection changed the course of human history. Jesus is the perfect fulfillment of all God's promises and covenants in the Old Testament. Jesus is the bridge between God and man. Jesus is the *only* way to God—and he is for all people for all time. This study will reveal many truths about Jesus; it will also challenge you to follow him, to lay down your life and pick up his cross. Jesus desires for each of us to carry on the mission he began.

ABOUT THE SESSIONS

Each session in this book is designed for group use—either in a small group setting or adult Sunday school class. The sessions contain enough material to keep your group busy for a full ninety-minute small group time but can also be easily adapted to work in a shorter meeting time—a true crash course. Or if you'd like to spend even more time, feel free to take two weeks for each of the six sessions; that essentially provides a quarter of a year's worth of content for your group.

The readings, activities, and discussion questions will help your group dig deeper into the Bible passages, engage in thought-provoking dialogue, explore ways to personally apply the material . . . and get to know one another better! Every group member should have a copy of *Crash Course on Jesus,* both for at-home readings and for use during group time. As you go through the study during your group time, take turns reading aloud the text and questions in the book. That gives everyone a sense of participating in the study together.

Here's how each session breaks down:

Launch

At the beginning of each session, you'll find a great introduction to the topic (be sure to read this aloud at the beginning of your meeting!), a list of Scriptures you'll study during the session, any extra supplies to bring, and notes on anything else to prepare before the session.

There's also a launching activity to start your group time. This activity sets the stage for the week's topic and gets people ready to start talking!

Explore

Next up is the meat of the study—the "Explore" section. This portion includes several teaching points that each focus on a specific aspect of the broader session topic. As you explore each teaching point, you'll study some Scripture passages, interact with one another as you talk through challenging questions, and read commentary on the passages. Also included are excerpts from related Christianity Today International articles (more about that below) that will enrich group discussion. If you are leading the group, be sure to ask God to help you make his Word come alive for your group during this time of exploring his truth (see Hebrews 4:12).

Apply

The Christian life—the abundant life—is about more than just thoughtful study and dialogue. James says, "As the body without the spirit is dead, so faith without deeds is dead" (James 2:26). The "Apply" section of each session will help take your discussion and study to another level; it will help you *live out* the ideas and values from that session. During this time, each participant will choose from three different challenge options (or come up with their own) to do during the coming week. These challenges will help group members make what they've learned a part of their lives in a practical way.

Pray

Before you finish up, be sure to take some time to pray for one another. In the "Pray" section, you'll find an idea you can use for your group's closing prayer.

Before Next Time

Take a look at the "Before Next Time" box for a heads-up on what to read or prepare for your next meeting.

FOR FURTHER RESEARCH

Resource List

Located at the end of session 6 is a list of recommended resources that can help take your study on the topic even further. You'll want to check those out!

Christianity Today International Articles

You'll also find three bonus articles from Christianity Today International publications. These articles are written by men who are well versed on Jesus' life and ministry. The sessions reference the articles during the course of the study. These articles are meant to help your group dive deeply into the topic and discuss a variety of facts, thoughts, and opinions. Taking the time to read these articles (as well as anything else suggested in the "Before Next Time" box at the end of each session) will greatly enrich your group's discussion and help you engage further with each topic.

It's our prayer that *Crash Course on Jesus* will change the lives of your group members as you come to better understand Jesus' birth, ministry, identity, death, resurrection, and promised return. May the Holy Spirit move in and through your group as you grow in your knowledge of and relationship with our Savior and Lord, Jesus Christ.

Miraculous Birth | 1

This beautiful and miraculous account reveals
God's sovereign plan for the redemption of his people.

Although the Lord Jesus Christ was born in Bethlehem, that was not the beginning of his existence. This is one of the ways in which he is absolutely unique and different from us. None of us existed before we were in our mothers' wombs. But for Jesus Christ it was different. Before he was conceived in the womb of the virgin Mary, the Bible tells us, his glory filled the heavens. "In the beginning was the Word [a name for Jesus], and the Word was with God, and the Word was God" (John 1:1). Since before the creation, before the beginning of time as we know it, God has always been God the Father, God the Son, and God the Holy Spirit. Christ was with God and he was God.

But then: "The Word became flesh and made his dwelling among us" (v. 14). God himself stooped to enter the world, to enter into human history, to redeem us by becoming one of us.

IHϯΛΝΤΟΔΙΕϹШοнΠΟϮΕΥΟΜΕΝΟΝϹ

LAUNCH

Read Luke 2:22-38.

Look at the printout of the fourteenth-century painting *Presentation in the Temple* by Italian artist Ambrogio Lorenzetti. What stands out to you in this painting? If you were going to depict Jesus as a baby, what would you do differently?

Why do you think it was significant that Jesus, the Son of God, entered the world as a tiny, helpless, human baby?

EXPLORE

Teaching Point One: Jesus' parents weren't chosen by accident.

Read Luke 1:26-38.

We can't read the account of the first Christmas without spending some time focusing on Mary, the mother of Jesus. Imagine her, in the midst of her morning chores, daydreaming about her future with Joseph. What kind of husband would he be? What would their children be like?

Suddenly, the unthinkable happened. The angel Gabriel appeared! If that weren't strange enough, he gave Mary an even stranger greeting. He called her "favored" and said, "The Lord is with you" (v. 28). She was baffled! Gabriel sensed her confusion and explained more: she would conceive and give birth to a child—the long-awaited Messiah.

Imagine the swirl of emotions. On one hand, she was stunned by the honor. On the other hand, she dreaded how this might play out. What would people think? Jewish law said that adultery was punishable by stoning. Yet Mary quickly chose to surrender: "I am the Lord's servant. . . . May it be to me as you have said" (v. 38). In simple faith, Mary said yes to God.

Something about Mary allowed her to surrender to God's will. What do you think that quality or characteristic was? If you had to sum up Mary's qualities in a single word, what word would you choose?

What did Mary have to give up to accept God's will for her life? What did she gain?

Have you ever had to surrender something to God and found it difficult? Explain. What was the hardest thing about it? What was the result?

Read Matthew 1:18-25.

When Mary learned she was pregnant with Jesus, she and Joseph weren't living together. They may not have even lived in the same village.

At first Joseph probably wondered whether Mary had been unfaithful. Surely he was devastated and heartbroken. He could have subjected her to public humiliation, but instead, because he was a righteous man, he had in mind to divorce her quietly. Had Joseph done this, he would have known that most people would assume that he was the father of Mary's child and that the divorce was caused by a reason other than adultery. Joseph was an honorable man who was willing to put his reputation at risk instead of Mary's.

However, an angel of the Lord revealed to Joseph that Mary had conceived her child by the Holy Spirit, and that this son was Jesus, the promised Messiah. Joseph courageously obeyed as the angel commanded. He took Mary home to be his wife, which also meant that he willingly claimed responsibility for the child. What do you admire most about Joseph in this account? What do you think this says about the man God chose to be Jesus' earthly father?

Put yourself in Joseph's place. How would you have felt if you faced this situation?

What did Joseph have to give up in order to accept God's will in his life? What did he gain?

Putting God's plan above their own is a defining characteristic of the people God has chosen to use throughout history. A sacrificial view of life leads to both beauty and pain. When have you felt God calling you to something bigger than your own plans? How have you responded?

Jesus' parents were not chosen by accident. God didn't randomly pick an engaged couple to raise Jesus. He chose two people who were willing to live by faith, two people who recognized that their lives were not their own but God's—to do with as he would. And in giving up their own plans for life, they became a central part in God's greater plan for redeeming his people.

Teaching Point Two: The story of Jesus' birth is miraculous, beautiful, and symbolic.

Read Luke 2:1-20.

Most of us have heard this account of Jesus' birth many, many times— the rhythm and language of this passage as familiar to us as Christmas morning. And being so familiar sometimes makes it seem commonplace. This story, though, is anything but common! There is danger, there is a journey, there are ordinary people chosen for an extraordinary mission, there are angels and shepherds. This is the beautiful and miraculous story of our Savior's birth.

No matter how many times you read it, what always amazes you about the Christmas story? What detail stood out to you this time that you haven't really noticed or thought about on previous readings?

Talk about the symbolism of various parts of this account: the census, the journey to Bethlehem, the birth in the stable (or cave), the shepherds, the angels. Why are these important parts of the Christmas story?

In the "Christ's Birth and Your Birth" article, read the "Jesus' Story" section through the paragraph following the carol (p. 71). What phrases of the carol do you find most meaningful? What feelings and emotions do those words trigger in you? Explain.

Why is it vital that Jesus was both wholly man and wholly God?

Teaching Point Three: Jesus' birth is a fulfillment of all that came before.
Read Matthew 1:1-17.

When most of us come to a long list of names in the Bible, we tend to skim quickly to get to whatever follows. Maybe we don't understand the power a genealogy can have.

In Matthew 1:1-17, we find a genealogy of Jesus. But this list of ancestors includes some names you wouldn't expect to see in a typical Jewish genealogy. Specifically, it includes Gentiles and women, and some of the women had a shady past—including Bathsheba (the wife of Uriah), an adulteress; Rahab, a prostitute and Gentile from Jericho; Tamar, who dressed as a prostitute and seduced her father-in-law; and Ruth, a godly woman but of the Moabite race the Jews despised.

This genealogy deserves a closer look, because in this brief list, Matthew not only includes forty-two generations of Jesus' descendants, he also traces Jesus' bloodline back to King David (and beyond to Abraham) to demonstrate Jesus' claim to the throne of Israel. This genealogy communicates a powerful truth: Jesus is the Messiah for all people; his kingdom includes Jews and Gentiles, men and women. This genealogy goes even further than that though; this list of names also shows us God's sovereign hand weaving his plan of redemption into the story of his people—from the very beginning.

Why do you think Matthew's genealogy includes prostitutes, adulterers, and other people considered second-class citizens by the Jewish people?

Read Galatians 3:28, 29. What would it have meant to the Galatians to hear Paul say, "There is neither Jew nor Greek, slave nor free, male nor female"? In what ways would this have been radical and life-changing for them?

How might you paraphrase Galatians 3:28, 29 for our world? What groups would you include?

Read Genesis 49:8-10 and 1 Samuel 16:1-13. How do these passages show God's plan for Jesus at work even generations before his birth? How do Jesus' birth, life, and death fulfill God's promises of the Old Testament?

 APPLY

So much of that first Christmas story is centered on humility. Jesus humbled himself and became a human. Mary and Joseph accepted God's call with humility and willingness—not counting the cost to their own lives. Jesus was born in the midst of poverty and shame in a no-name village, to young parents (probably outcasts due to Mary's pregnancy), and with a feeding trough as a makeshift cradle. Even Jesus' genealogy is humble in nature—filled with names no one would claim: Gentiles, adulterers, murderers.

Jesus did not come to earth in glory and splendor. He came humbly. Paul exhorts us to live with this same humility: "Your attitude should be the same as that of Christ Jesus: Who, being in very nature God, did not consider equality with God something to be grasped, but made himself nothing, taking the very nature of a servant, being made in human likeness. And being found in appearance as a man, he humbled himself and became obedient to death—even death on a cross!" (Philippians 2:5-8).

Choose one of the following application options to do on your own this week. Turn to a partner and share your choice.

JESUS—MAN AND GOD

Search online for art and other media that depict Jesus' birth. One source worth checking out is www.goodsalt.com. What false images do these media portray? What "real" things do they communicate? Print out one that most communicates Jesus' humanity to you and use it as a bookmark in your Bible until next Christmas. Each time you see it, spend a few moments thanking God for coming to earth in human form to establish a relationship with you.

UNFILTERED

"I am the Lord's servant," Mary answered. "May it be to me as you have said." With Mary, everything was directed away from herself to what God would do through her and in her. Medieval artists often portrayed Mary in stained-glass windows. Her pane would be the only one with no color in it. Clear glass. All the other windowpanes would filter the light of the sun through their own distinctive designs. Mary was clear, unfiltered. There was nothing of herself to affect the light that came through. She did not advance herself, but advanced the work of God.

Paint a "stained glass" picture of yourself. Through what do you filter God's call on your life? Is it your job? your talents? your family? your hopes for the future? Now paint a clear, unfiltered picture of yourself. Pray that God would remove the filters you place between you and him; ask that God would help you advance the work of God, not yourself or your own desires.

DO A GENEALOGY

You might have a family member who has already done some genealogy searches. Or you can poke around online, using search terms such as *free genealogy*. You might start by simply listing yourself and then work backward and record your siblings, parents, aunts, uncles, cousins, grandparents, etc. You can add the word *forms* to your search to download free forms that will help you. Once you've done some research this week, think about the surprises you find among your ancestors. Do you find mostly "sinners," or "saints"? What do the people in your family history show you about how God works in people's lives?

 ## PRAY

Break into groups of three during your closing prayer time. If possible, hold hands as you pray. Pray for specific personal requests; then thank God for sending Jesus to earth in human form to identify with us. Ask God to help each of you sense that he's still just as close and real and personal as the people whose hands you're holding.

> BEFORE NEXT TIME: *Read "Come Die with Me" by Daniel Meyer (p. 87) to prepare for next week's session. The leader should gather recent copies of celebrity magazines (such as* Us, People, Entertainment Weekly, *and* OK!*) and news magazines (*Time, Newsweek*) to use in the "Launch" activity.*

Radical Ministry | 2

The greatest teacher of all time delivers a
tough message of radical discipleship.

While the entire Bible can teach us practical, godly ways to live, we're especially fortunate that God guided the four writers of the Gospels to preserve many of Jesus' teachings during his earthly ministry.

Like the disciples and other followers of Jesus' day whom he taught directly, we can figuratively sit at his feet and learn from what he taught. And we can apply it directly to our lives as his followers and his representatives to the world today.

While it would take a lifetime to fully explore all of Jesus' rich teachings from the time he lived and ministered on earth, today we'll focus on three important messages that Jesus both taught and lived out: loving others with no boundaries, avoiding stubborn legalism, and living with the kingdom always in mind.

BIBLE BASIS: *Micah 6:8; Matthew 12:1-14; 16:26; 18:21-35; 22:34-39; 23:15, 23-28; 24:36-44; 28:16-20; Mark 7:1-23; Luke 6:27-36; 10:1-37; 23:32-34; John 10:10; 15:1-17; 21:15-19*

EXTRA SUPPLIES: *celebrity and news magazines*

LAUNCH

Break into groups of three or four participants. In each group, look through a few magazines and identify some examples of people living contrary to Jesus' teachings and some examples of people following Jesus' teachings. Then discuss these questions:

In general, what does the world's attitude seem to be toward Jesus' teachings about life?

In what ways does Jesus call us to live counterculturally? What are the difficulties with that? What are the benefits?

EXPLORE

Teaching Point One: Jesus calls us to a deeper level of human relationship.

Read Matthew 22:34-39; Luke 6:27-36 and 10:25-37.

Love God and love people. Jesus said, in essence, that this is everything the law is about. But Jesus didn't leave it at that. He was constantly challenging people to expand, to reach out beyond where they were comfortable, to love further and harder and longer and more. His messages clearly teach that you can help and influence not only the people you know or the people who are just like you. You can look beyond your backyard to see the people and the needs in your city and country . . . and yes, the world. It's not about who is like you, whom you approve of, or who can repay you. Love should not be bound by danger, culture, or stigma.

And Jesus pushed the boundaries of our love even further than that, beyond where most of us would ever go or imagine going if left on our own. He said to love your enemies too.

How do these passages demonstrate the radical love to which Jesus calls us?

The Samaritan loved across all sorts of boundaries. How is his story the epitome of Jesus' teachings on love?

Who (or what type of person) is hard for you to love? Why? How do these verses inspire and challenge you in that relationship?

Read Matthew 18:21-35; Luke 23:32-34 and John 21:15-19.

Jesus understood that in the course of all human relationships there would be hurt and betrayal. But just as he called us to *love* radically, Jesus also calls us to *forgive* radically—something he not only demonstrated in his teachings but also in his life and death. Why is forgiveness such a critical component of loving others?

When has someone hurt you in exactly the same way over and over? How do you feel about forgiving that person endlessly (seventy-seven times) for that same sin?

Think of a time when you forgave someone. How did that act of forgiveness affect the relationship?

Jesus not only forgave Peter's betrayal, he also reinstated Peter and gave him a mission. Why were those additional steps important?

What do you find most radical about Jesus' call to forgive?

Read John 15:1-17.

Jesus is our example for radical love and radical forgiveness—and his example led all the way to death. "Greater love has no one than this, that he lay down his life for his friends" (v. 13). Jesus calls us to a level of love and relationship that we cannot do on our own. It's why he tells us in these verses that we must remain in him, that apart from him we can do nothing (v. 5). A radical love can come only from an outflow of our relationship with Jesus. It is the result of his radical love for us, first.

Teaching Point Two: Jesus teaches that following him is about more than rules.

Read Matthew 12:1-14; 23:23-28 and Mark 7:1-23.

Jesus' most accusatory teachings were not directed to the sinners you'd expect: drunkards, tax collectors, adulterers . . . Instead he reserved his harshest words for the "righteous" Pharisees who were poisoning God's people with their burdensome rules and impossible traditions.

Jesus called them a "brood of vipers" (Matthew 23:33) and accused them of making their converts twice as much the sons of Hell as they were (v. 15). Ouch!

Jesus didn't pull any punches with these men. They had made the life of faith into one of legalism and rule-abiding. They weren't paying attention to people's hearts. For them it had become about *appearing* to look good instead of about actually *being* good.

Jesus reminded them over and over again that it wasn't about human traditions, stubborn legalism, or appearances. It was about acting justly, loving mercy, and walking humbly with God (Micah 6:8).

What common message did you hear Jesus preaching to the Pharisees in these three passages?

Why do you think Jesus was so tough on the Pharisees but seemed to let other more blatant sinners off the hook?

How are you convicted by Jesus' words to the Pharisees? In what ways might you be living like a Pharisee? How are you challenged to reevaluate your own life and faith in light of Jesus' message in these passages?

Teaching Point Three: Jesus wants us to live with a sense of urgency, mindful of his coming kingdom.

Read Matthew 24:36-44; 28:16-20 and Luke 10:1-24.

What is the harvest? Why is it so important for us to be harvesting now?

Jesus referred to the days of Noah when talking about his second coming: "In the days before the flood, people were eating and drinking, marrying and giving in marriage, up to the day Noah entered the ark" (Matthew 24:38). These things are not bad things—they are the stuff of every day—but they are not *the point* of life. What do you want the point of your life to be? What do you want to be doing when the Son of Man comes?

How do these passages convict you in your relationships? your work? How do they give you meaning and purpose?

Read Matthew 16:26.

Read the first three paragraphs of the section "Someone Must Die" in Daniel Meyer's article "Come Die With Me" (p. 88). What additional impact do Meyer's words bring to Jesus' question in Matthew 16:26: "What good will it be for a man if he gains the whole world, yet forfeits his soul?"

Read John 10:10. What did Jesus mean when he said that he came to bring us a full life? What do you think a full life looks like?

How can you focus more on living for eternity? How might God use your present circumstances to achieve eternal goals?

APPLY

Jesus calls us to a life of radical discipleship. He teaches us to abandon our boundaries on love, our stubborn grip on cultural traditions and rules, and our pursuit of "the good life." The life Jesus calls us to is a full life—an abundant one—but it is one of self-sacrifice, one that pursues Jesus and his coming kingdom at all cost.

The teachings of Jesus are not easy, they're not soft, and they're not feel-good clichés. They challenge the heart and core of human selfishness, but they also prod us to a deeper life, an exciting one filled with mission and purpose.

Choose one of the following application options to do on your own this week. Turn to a partner and share your choice.

BE A FRIEND

Perhaps a specific person came to mind when your group discussed Jesus' teaching on love and forgiveness. If so, what aspects of your life do you need to work on to accept, forgive, or be more loyal to this friend? This week, ask your friend to join you for coffee or lunch. During your face-to-face time, focus on changing your own attitude and following Christ's example of radical love. This needs to come as an outflow of your own love for Christ. Reread John 15:1-17 before you meet with your friend.

TURN AWAY

Reread Matthew 23:23-28 and Mark 7:1-23. Think about the ways you try to keep up your outside appearance to look good to the world: your job, your physical looks, your house, maybe even your service at church and your giving. Make a list and then consider the inside, your heart. What attitudes and actions belie your outside appearance? How are you hypocritical? What elements of outside appearance might you need to give up in order to tend to what's on the inside? Pray about these things and consider confiding in a trusted friend or counselor as you strive to make these inward changes.

LOSE IT!

What could you give away? What could you do without? What could you give up for the sake of eternity? A good place to start might be as simple as giving up one hour of TV to serve a neighbor by mowing his lawn or shoveling his driveway. Make a chart with one column labeled "give up" and a second column labeled "replace with." Ask God to help you see both what you can sacrifice and what to replace it with in order to serve him. Then take action!

 # PRAY

Break into pairs. Before you pray, spend a few minutes sharing with each other the area of Jesus' teaching discussed today that you found most meaningful. In pairs, spend time praying for God to help each of you experience being the kind of person that Jesus described in his teachings. Ask God to reveal fresh and practical ways that each of us can live out Jesus' teachings of radical love, interior purity, and kingdom-mindedness.

BEFORE NEXT TIME: *Read "Zacchaeus" by Earl Palmer (p. 78) to prepare for next week's session. The leader should do (or assign someone to do) a general online search using the phrase* unusual job titles *or* funny job titles. *You should find dozens of unusual job titles, including things like Master of Madness, Lord High Pencil Sharpener, and Decider-in-Chief. Print out some of your favorites (ten or so) for the "Launch" activity. Also do an online search for titles of Jesus. Print that out and bring it to your group for the closing prayer time.*

Divine Identity | 3

Jesus is the Son of God, our great teacher
and leader, our Messiah, our Savior.

Of all the people admired in the world today, Jesus of Nazareth continually ranks at the top of the list. Even those who don't call themselves Christians regard Jesus as one of the wisest teachers and most loving leaders the world has ever known. He is still making the covers of magazines and being talked about in coffee shops like no other person who has walked this earth.

So why did his contemporaries kill him? What was it about what he said or did that was so provoking and upsetting that religious and secular leaders alike wanted to see him dead? What was it about Jesus that could make the crowds that once followed him finally turn on him, demanding his blood and cheering about his pain? What was it about this man who, centuries later, is still worshiped by so many—and remains a controversial figure for so many others?

ΤΟΥΚΑΙΕΣΕΛΘΩΝΕΚΕΙΟΣΝΦΛΟΝΕ

> **BIBLE BASIS:** *Isaiah 9:6; Matthew 28:18-20; John 1:1-51; 2:13-17; 6:32-43; 13:1-5, 14, 15; 14:6*
>
> **EXTRA SUPPLIES:** *list of unusual job titles and list of the titles of Jesus*

LAUNCH

Name some unusual or unique job titles you've heard before. Take a look at the list of crazy job titles that was brought in. Then as a group discuss the following questions:

What do you think a person's job title says about what he or she does? What's your job title? What other titles do you have (student, husband, homeowner, neighbor)? What do these titles say about identity?

What are some of Jesus' titles? What do they say about his identity?

EXPLORE

Teaching Point One: Jesus' identity is beyond human expectation.

Read Isaiah 9:6 and John 1:1-51.

As we follow Jesus' story through Scripture, we see that he is the demonstration and ultimate revelation of who God is. From the first words of

ΙΗ✝ΑΝΤΟΔΙΕCѠ°ᴴΠΟΡΕΥΟΜΕΝΟΝ

the Old Testament and continuing even until today, Jesus' story is all about how God's people must choose either to embrace or reject who he is.

By looking at the titles Jesus is given in Scripture, we can understand more about his identity and the way he works to reconcile us to God.

Name the titles given to Jesus in these passages. What do you think these titles teach about him?

When you think of Christ, how do you perceive him and why? In what ways does the image you have compare with the titles given to Jesus in these passages?

Which of the titles from these passages do you most desire Jesus to fulfill in your life right now? Why?

The title the Jews of Jesus' day most wanted Jesus to fulfill was that of the promised Messiah. Yet in the article "Zacchaeus," Earl Palmer states that by the time Jesus met Zacchaeus the tax collector, the crowds were upset because Jesus wasn't fulfilling their expectations of what this Messiah should be. Read the paragraph that begins on the bottom of page 82. Palmer adds: "One of the most elegant and most incredible proofs of our Lord's messiahship is how wonderfully he both fulfills and disappoints every expectation we have" (p. 83). What do you think he means? How did Jesus both fulfill and disappoint the expectations inherent in the other titles from these Scriptures? Explain ways or instances when this has been true in your life.

Teaching Point Two: Jesus is a strong but humble leader.

Read John 2:13-17.

Even when Jesus was surrounded by men who wanted to kill him, he stood up for God. He was a courageous leader who inspired and influenced his followers to boldly stand for God too. When you think of a leader, what attributes and character traits come to mind? How does Jesus display those characteristics in this passage?

What about Jesus' actions and words in this passage makes you want to follow him? What do you think Jesus wanted his followers to take away from this exchange?

Read John 13:1-5.

Jesus influenced others with his compassion and humility. He was the Son of God, yet he came to serve. His model is more than simply one of a servant leader—he was a sacrificial leader. He put everyone above himself and ultimately gave his life for the sake of his people.

Have you ever worked for someone who put himself or herself before everyone else? Describe how that person made you feel.

At the end of this passage, Jesus told his disciples, "Now that I, your Lord and Teacher, have washed your feet, you also should wash one another's feet. I have set you an example that you should do as I have done for you" (vv. 14, 15). What was he trying to communicate?

How can you follow Jesus' example and model this kind of servanthood?

Read Matthew 28:18-20.

In addition to being a courageous and sacrificial leader, Jesus was also a visionary leader. Shortly before his return to Heaven, he cast perhaps his greatest vision in what we call the Great Commission. What qualities does Jesus display in these verses that show he is a visionary leader? What do you think caused this vision to so take hold in the hearts and minds of the apostles that they would be willing even to die for it?

Teaching Point Three: Jesus is the way, the truth, and the life.

Read John 6:32-43 and 14:6.

Jesus is our only hope for restoration and salvation with God. No one else can fulfill this role of Messiah and Savior. Jesus alone is wholly human, wholly God, and wholly sinless. He alone is the perfect sacrifice, completely satisfying the debt for our sins. There is no other way to God the Father, no other way to eternal life in Heaven. Jesus alone is the way, the truth, and the life.

Jesus called himself "the bread of life" (v. 35) and said that anyone who looks to him will have eternal life. How is Christ "enough" in your life; how does he satisfy you? What happens in your life when you turn to other things for satisfaction? List some practical ways you can set aside these things of the world and turn to Jesus to bring you fulfillment.

Why is Jesus the only way to eternal life? What makes that so troublesome for people today to understand and accept? Why do you believe it?

How is your identity as a Christian rooted in the identity of Jesus?

 APPLY

Jesus was much more than meek and mild. He was more than a poetic philosopher. Jesus was the light of Heaven hitting a darkened earth like a meteor blast. He made claims and demands that left people undone. He named realities that others sought to bury. He broke barriers and battered bastions no one else had the nerve to assault. He called for the utter dismantling of the way things were and the new creation of something so much better. Jesus was not politically correct. He was not religiously pious. He was not socially tame. Jesus was a dangerous man because he was, and is, the God who is dangerously good.

Do we know this Jesus, and does it show? Or has our concept of Jesus become so domesticated that he no longer really disturbs us, no longer really disrupts us, no longer really disciples us into the new life of the kingdom of God?

Choose one of the following application options to do on your own this week. Turn to a partner and share your choice.

A MISSING PIECE

Reread Isaiah 9:6 and John 1:1-51. Which of Jesus' titles are you most comfortable with? How do you generally perceive and relate to Jesus? This week, make a conscious effort to see and worship Jesus in a different role. For example, how is Jesus the Wonderful Counselor in your life? What does it mean that Jesus is the Prince of Peace? How are these roles *all* essential parts of Jesus' identity?

LEADING INFLUENCE

Is Christ your leader? When do you most resist Christ's leadership? Make a chart of all the areas in your life: family, job, school, disciplines, friendships. Pray through each of them and ask Jesus to be your leader in those areas. Think about what type of leadership you need in each department: courageous leadership, visionary leadership, or sacrificial leadership. Ask Jesus to help you submit to his leadership in all areas of your life.

MAKE A MEAL

What's your favorite meal? What's your favorite "comfort food"? Meat loaf and mashed potatoes, Thanksgiving dinner with all the trimmings . . . ? How does that meal satisfy you? Now list the ways that Jesus satisfies you. How can you make the menu that Jesus offers more practical, visible, or tangible in your everyday life?

# PRAY

Use the list of titles for Jesus that your group created on page 30 and any additional titles that your leader found in an online search. Spend time in silent prayer. Your leader will prompt by reading one of Jesus' titles (and if possible, a brief description or a related verse of Scripture from the online search). Silently ask God to make Jesus more real to you in that way.

BEFORE NEXT TIME: *Group members should each bring in one or two images of the cross—carvings, paintings, jewelry, or photos. The leader should also bring in palm branches or substitutes; you can use other large leaves from ferns, purchase artificial palm or fern branches, or make palm branches from a pattern (search online using the words* palm branch pattern*). If opting to have a Communion service during the "Explore" section, the leader should bring those materials.*

Sacrificial Death | 4

Despite rejection and the cross,
Jesus is exalted as king.

In the Christian faith, the cross symbolizes Jesus' death. Yet like many aspects of our faith, the symbol sometimes becomes just that—only a symbol.

If we want our faith—and the amazing gift of salvation that God offers us—to be more than a mere symbol, we must place the death of Christ on the cross at the very center of what we believe.

Most of us find it much easier to focus on other aspects of Jesus' ministry and life rather than on the most essential, if gruesome, part—that he came to die for us.

In this study, we'll look at how Jesus set the stage for his crucifixion and sacrifice through the elements of the Passover meal at the last supper. We'll also take a brutal look at the many rejections of Jesus that define the crucifixion. We will discover the eternal *promises inherent in Jesus' sacrificial death. And finally, we'll explore our response to Jesus' death—his call to take up our own crosses and share in his sufferings.*

BIBLE BASIS: *Exodus 6:6, 7; 24:6-8; Deuteronomy 21:23; Psalm 22:18; 69:21; Isaiah 53:12; Amos 8:9, 10; Matthew 16:24, 25; 26:17-30; 27:11-25, 27-54; John 12:12, 13*

EXTRA SUPPLIES: *images of the cross, palm branches or substitutes, Communion materials (if doing that option in "Explore")*

BEFOREHAND: *The leader should arrange things for the Communion service (if having). The leader may want to alert two readers to be prepared for the "Pray" activity.*

LAUNCH

Break into groups of four or five people. Share the images of the cross you've brought and discuss the following in your small groups:

Why is the cross the focal point of Christianity?

As you look at the various images of the cross in front of you, do you think the use of the cross in jewelry and in other images—including even those in churches—has watered down what it represents? Explain.

 EXPLORE

Teaching Point One: Communion sets the stage for Jesus' death and sacrifice.

Read Matthew 26:17-30 and Exodus 6:6, 7.

Jesus based Communion on the Passover Feast (Matthew 26:17-19) that for fifteen hundred years had been teaching God's people man's great need and God's great salvation. This sacred observance looked back to God's deliverance of the Israelites from the slavery of Egypt and the plague of death on all the firstborn in that land.

It was a meal of strange recipes and flavors—saltwater to remind people of the tears of slavery; bitter herbs, like horseradish, so people would remember the sour flavor of bondage; a fruit paste with cinnamon sticks to remind people of making bricks of clay and straw; a meal of lamb, commemorating how a lamb was killed for every household and its blood sprinkled on the doorposts, signaling the angel of death to pass over; flat bread, made without yeast, to remind God's people that they are to be both holy (no yeast, signifying sin puffing up their hearts) and ready to travel (such bread could be made quickly, would travel well, and wouldn't spoil).

Additionally, there were four cups of wine consumed throughout the meal. This custom was drawn from four promises made by God to Israel in Exodus 6:6, 7: "I will bring you out . . . I will free you from being slaves . . . I will redeem you . . . I will take you as my own people, and I will be your God."

To this day, Communion is more precious to us when we realize that we taste the ancient recipes of God's redemption and freedom. Jesus brought his disciples to the Passover meal on the eve of his death so that their taste for salvation would be piqued.

How did Passover prepare Israel's heart for Jesus' coming?

What is the significance of the body and the blood in Communion? Why do you think Jesus focused on those two elements in his sacrifice?

What goes through your mind when you take Communion?

Look again at Matthew 26:26-29. This meal feeds our deepest hunger, first because we yearn for food that will sustain us through all of life. Jesus' broken body is food for our journey. There is a reason Jesus chose bread as the symbol of his body. Bread made without yeast is a biblical symbol of holiness, yeast being an image of all that puffs up and ultimately spoils. Jesus is, for us, like dining on holiness. He is a food for our souls that never spoils, that only strengthens us, that nourishes righteousness and grace deep within us.

God required the Israelites to make unleavened bread so that they would have food for their journey out of bondage and into freedom. Here was bread that would last and not spoil, bread that was perfect for pilgrims, a precursor of manna (see Exodus 16). Jesus is that for us as well—food for our journey to the land of God's promises, food for the wilderness we must all pass through.

Because we hunger for God, the blood Jesus poured out for forgiveness seals our covenant with him (vv. 27, 28). Here Jesus took his disciples back to their memory of Exodus 24:6-8, when Moses secured Israel's commitment to God's covenant. Once again, blood would be shed and a covenant established between God and people, but this covenant is written on hearts and purchased with the blood of God's Son. This cup was the third of the four Passover cups, the cup of redemption, celebrating God's promise, "I will redeem you with an outstretched arm and with mighty acts of judgment" (Exodus 6:6). Who would have guessed that God's mighty act of judgment would be pronounced against his own Son, or that this redemption would purchase people for God from every tribe and language, people and nation?

Because we hunger for hope, this meal carries the promise of eternity with Christ. Many believe that Jesus had the fourth cup in mind when he said, "I tell you, I will not drink of this fruit of the vine from now on until that day when I drink it anew with you in my Father's kingdom" (v. 29). The fourth cup marked God's promise, "I will take you as my own people, and I will be your God" (Exodus 6:7). Down through the centuries until this day, the Passover liturgy, the Haggadah, repeats words like these: "This year we eat it in the land of bondage; next year in the land of promise." In our one Communion cup are contained both the promise of redemption and the promise of reunion. The promises sustain us.

How have you experienced Jesus as both sustaining bread and redeeming wine? How does the act of Communion reveal God's promises?

If you planned on celebrating Communion together, do so now.

Teaching Point Two: Jesus was utterly rejected as the Messiah-king.

Read Matthew 27:27-50.

Jesus had already felt the heavy blows of rejection through Judas's betrayal, Peter's denial, the disciples' abandonment, the courts that found him guilty of blasphemy, and the crowd crying for his crucifixion. Now the descent continued.

The Roman soldiers dramatized mankind's rejection of Jesus as king (vv. 27-31). They played a sadistic game with Jesus, outfitting him like a king but with a cast-off robe, a crown of thorns, a reed scepter, and a mocking tribute: "Hail, king of the Jews!"

Every deed that surrounded the crucifixion shouts rejection. Verses 32-38 provide a tightly packed summary according to the Old Testament script. Jesus was taken outside the holy city, rejected by his people like the sin offerings in Deuteronomy. He was offered wine mixed with gall, which tasted like bile. Some think this was a merciful narcotic, but more likely it was another mocking rejection, as predicted in Psalm 69:21: "They put gall in my food and gave me vinegar for my thirst."

He was crucified, the signal of God's curse according to Deuteronomy 21:23: "Anyone who is hung on a tree is under God's curse."

His clothes were confiscated, leaving him nothing, but fulfilling the prediction of Psalm 22:18, a psalm of the Messiah's rejection: "They divide my garments among them and cast lots for my clothing."

And they crucified him between two terrorists or robbers, as predicted in Isaiah 53:12: "[He] was numbered with the transgressors." Rejection was written on every act that surrounded Jesus' death; apparently no one saw that this was the suffering servant of Israel prophesied by Isaiah.

Added to these *deeds* of rejection was the crowd's *words* of ridicule in Matthew 27:39-44. In essence, these taunts said:

- "You can't build a new temple. Why, you can't even save yourself."
- "You aren't the king of Israel. You can't even come off this Roman cross."
- "You aren't the Son of God, because God won't save you. God doesn't want you!"

To think that such things were said to him who is one with the Father, to the one who is the Son of God!

Then came the hammer blow: Jesus was forsaken by God the Father (vv. 45-49). The darkness from noon till three o'clock signaled that God's own court was in session. Dark drapes were pulled around the proceedings. It was both too holy and too terrible for our eyes. The darkness was a familiar portent of God's judgment. Listen to the ominous prediction of Amos 8:9, 10: "'In that day,' declares the Sovereign LORD, 'I will make the sun go down at noon and darken the earth in broad daylight. I will turn your religious feasts into mourning and all your singing into weeping. I will make all of you wear sackcloth and shave your heads. I will make that time like mourning for an only son and the end of it like a bitter day.'"

Jesus' cry of desperation, "My God, my God, why have you forsaken me?" climaxed his abandonment. God the Father forsook God the Son because the judge would not look upon the sin-bearer. In those moments Jesus was no longer spotless; he was thoroughly stained with our sin. God the Father could not even face him. That was the ultimate price Jesus paid for our sins, a brief separation from his Father for our sakes.

When all this rejection came to the crushing finale with the Father's own rejection, when Jesus had suffered *from* sin and *for* sin . . . when it was all accomplished, "he gave up his spirit" (v. 50).

He died *from* sin and *for* sin. The charge of the mockers hangs in the air: "He saved others," they said, "but he can't save himself!" But Jesus did not come to save himself; he came to save us all.

Imagine that you were one of Jesus' followers that day. Why do you think they failed to see him as the suffering servant prophesied in Isaiah 53?

In what way is an act of sacrifice more powerful than an act of force?

Why was Jesus so willing to give up his life when everyone, including God the Father, had forsaken him?

Teaching Point Three: When Jesus died, rejected as king, he inaugurated a new kingdom of life.

Read Matthew 27:51-54.

In these verses Matthew records some amazing events. Each was a sign of the life that Jesus had secured. In verse 51, the torn veil in the temple signaled that forever after, forgiven sinners could go boldly to God without fear. The temple would continue to be in use for nearly another forty years, but in that moment it was essentially obsolete. All it represented had been torn down, just as Jesus had promised. No more sacrifices were needed. The priests all became unnecessary; they were just going through the motions. The great festivals were fulfilled.

By being rejected as Messiah-king, Jesus opened the way to God and closed the door forever on the old ways. Have you found forgiveness for your sins? You were forgiven because the veil is torn. Did you pray this week? You were heard because the veil was torn when Jesus died. Did you enjoy the Lord's company, his grace and truth? It was so because the veil is torn. Did you think of your heavenly home? It will be yours because the veil is torn!

Look again at verses 51-53. Isn't that wild! Many Bible scholars think our English translation needs to be repunctuated here, to indicate that while there was an earthquake when Jesus died, the bodies of the holy people were not resurrected until after Jesus' own resurrection. But the amazing point here is this rash of resurrections!

Here is the thing: the seemingly powerless Savior was mighty enough in his death to break open the dungeons of the dead. Look closely at these strange holy people. Just like us, they had trusted God for this moment, never imagining quite how extraordinary it would be. This hints at our own future—saints walking out of death, into the Holy City, testimonies of the power of Christ's life to all we meet in that eternal home.

The centurion and soldiers in verse 54 are the same governor's soldiers who so abused Jesus, who mocked him as king and crucified him as a criminal. And now: "Surely he was the Son of God!"

What details strike you most about this narrative?

What do you think was the significance of all those resurrections?

Why was the testimony of the centurion and soldiers so powerful?

APPLY

Read the last three paragraphs of the section "Someone Must Die" in Daniel Meyer's article "Come Die with Me" (p. 89).

Matthew 16:24, 25 gets quoted often—even in secular settings. What do you think Jesus' words mean here?

Meyer claims that the "death Christ calls for is a price entirely worth paying." Do you agree or disagree? Explain.

The *NLT* translates Matthew 16:24, 25 as follows: "If any of you wants to be my follower, you must turn from your selfish ways, take up your cross, and follow me. If you try to hang on to your life, you will lose it. But if you give up your life for my sake, you will save it." What selfish ways do you need to turn from? What practical steps can you take? How will your life change?

Choose one of the following application options to do on your own this week. Turn to a partner and share your choice.

AT THE CROSS

Create a cross bookmark. Make this as simple or as artistic as you like. On the cross, write verses, questions, answers, or other thoughts from today's session that stood out. Place the bookmark in your Bible—

you'll be surprised at times when God prompts you to read the thoughts you've recorded.

COMMUNION QUESTIONS

Read 1 Corinthians 11:27-32. Paul warned that we shouldn't take Communion in an unworthy manner. That doesn't mean that sinners can't eat this meal—after all, we're all sinners. But it does mean that each of us must invite the Lord's examination. Come up with a list of questions you can ask yourself to examine your heart before you take Communion. Tuck this list into your Bible, and silently read through it the next time you take part in the Lord's Supper. Ask God to remove any obstacles to enjoying a complete relationship with him.

MAKE A COMMITMENT

How should you respond to Jesus' death on the cross for you? Do you need to accept his forgiveness and proclaim him Lord of your life? Do you need to commit your life to his service as a result of his sacrifice for you? If you have previously made that commitment, evaluate the current direction of your life. Does it reflect gratitude for Jesus' sacrifice? discipleship in his ways? Take some moments for quiet reflection. If you feel comfortable doing so, call or e-mail a few group members and ask them to pray about your conclusions.

 # PRAY

Each participant should hold a palm branch (or substitute). As the leader reads John 12:12, 13, participants should wave their palm branches in the air, and shout on the leader's cue: "Hosanna! Blessed is he who comes in the name of the Lord! Blessed is the King of Israel!"

Put down the palm branches. Now for a dramatization of Matthew 27:11-25, begin with one volunteer (narrator) reading verses 11-20 from the Bible. Then the dialogue from verses 21-25 can be read using the abbreviated printed text below—with another reader acting as Pilate and the rest of the group members shouting the angry words of the crowd (in bold).

"Which of the two do you want me to release to you?"

"Barabbas!"

"What shall I do, then, with Jesus who is called Christ?"

"Crucify him!"

"Why? What crime has he committed?"

"Crucify him!"

"I am innocent of this man's blood. It is your responsibility!"

"Let his blood be on us and on our children!"

We're no different from the people of Jesus' day. Just as we might have shouted "Hosanna!" we also might have screamed "Crucify him!"

Have a brief time of silent prayer. One member can close with a prayer focusing on the fact that we often fail both to recognize Jesus as king and to grasp how much we needed Jesus' death, the only path to our salvation.

BEFORE NEXT TIME: *Read the different accounts of Jesus' resurrection in Matthew 28; Mark 16; Luke 24 and John 20, 21. The leader should prepare to bring (or assign someone to bring): for the "Launch" activity— a round balloon (white preferred), #2 pencil, and index card for each member, plus wet wipes; for the "Pray" time—small bells, colored paper or colored banners.*

Glorious Resurrection | 5

The evidence is overwhelming
that Jesus rose from the dead.

"He is risen!"

Can you imagine the emotions of the disciples on that first Easter morning? The joy. The confusion. The fear. The hesitant excitement. The vague memory of Jesus' words: "They will condemn [the Son of Man] to death and will hand him over to the Gentiles, who will mock him and spit on him, flog him and kill him. Three days later he will rise" (Mark 10:33, 34).

Could it really be true?

The resurrection is at the center of our faith, and we must grab hold of it and believe it fully and completely. But this shouldn't be done glibly or without thought. We must examine the evidence for ourselves.

BIBLE BASIS: *Matthew 27:57–28:15; Mark 10:33, 34; John 11:25; 1 Corinthians 15:1-8, 12-20*

EXTRA SUPPLIES: *for "Launch"—a round balloon (white preferred), #2 pencil, and index card for each member, plus wet wipes; for "Pray"— small bells, colored paper or colored banners*

BEFOREHAND: *The leader should blow up the balloons (to roughly the size of baseballs) and loosely tie them for use during the "Launch" activity.*

LAUNCH

Each group member needs a balloon, a #2 pencil, and an index card. First, take a pencil, place it at an angle against the index card, and fill up about half the card with graphite as if you're shading in a drawing. Press your fingers and thumb onto the pencil graphite on the index card, as you would to take fingerprints. Then make fingerprints on your balloon. Use the wipes to clean your hands.

In groups of three or four participants, compare your fingerprints. If you want, you can untie the balloons and blow them up to enlarge your prints. Then discuss these questions:

Why are fingerprints iconic for evidence collecting? Look around the room. How many of your fingerprints do you think are here? What other evidence is there that you have been here today?

What kind of evidence for or against Jesus' resurrection do you think exists? What could prove beyond a shadow of a doubt that Jesus did physically rise from the dead?

 EXPLORE

Teaching Point One: The resurrection is not a fabricated myth.
Read 1 Corinthians 15:1-8.

First Corinthians 15 is one of the earliest records of the resurrection of Jesus. The letter to the Corinthians is dated between AD 52 and 55. If Jesus died when he was thirty-three years old, that means this letter was written roughly twenty years after Jesus' resurrection.

Some critics say that the events of the Bible were written so long after they actually took place that mythology developed around that writing. That could not be. Not enough time had gone by for that to happen. Look at what Paul said in verse 6. He said that the resurrected Christ appeared to more than five hundred people at one time, "most of whom are still living." In other words, "You can go ask them if you care to check it out."

Even the most skeptical theologians agree that Paul was the writer of this letter to the Corinthians, and we know that he was writing to them just five years after he had visited them. Paul didn't meet Jesus until five years after Jesus' resurrection. So Paul is recounting to the Corinthians something that occurred only a dozen or so years before. Think back to the last dozen years of your own life to consider what a short amount of time that is.

According to this passage, what were the essential messages of the gospel?

Why do you think Paul listed so many people who had seen Jesus after his resurrection?

What doubts have you had about the resurrection? Why must we be convinced of Jesus' resurrection in order to properly worship him?

Teaching Point Two: Evidence proves the tomb was empty.

Read Matthew 27:57–28:15.

Some critics reject the Christian faith on the basis that the resurrection of Jesus was some mythological story put together by bereaved followers. For instance, one idea is called the swoon theory. It says that Jesus' followers drugged him with the wine he took when he was on the cross, which resulted in the guards thinking he was dead. And even though he'd been beaten half to death, nailed through his hands and feet, speared through his side, torn off the cross, and stuck in a stone-cold tomb, he survived.

Suppose that were true. Three days unattended in a cold tomb would surely wipe him out. But suppose he survived that; and then somebody stole his body, and he revived afterwards. Do you think those who stole the body would have been convinced that this Jesus—bedraggled, beat up, half dead, obviously a mere human—was the Messiah? Would they have then been willing to die for what they knew to be a lie? Tradition tells us that most of them were later brutally executed. A lie might be perpetrated for some profit, but not if it costs your life. Surely one of the disciples would have cracked under the pressure. And what was supposed to have happened to Jesus? Did he remain in hiding while all his followers died? What would be the point?

There's another theory: the body was stolen by the Pharisees. Now *that* we can understand. They'd heard Jesus promise he would be resurrected from the dead. So in order to make sure that didn't happen, they stole the body. But once the word got out that his disciples were misrepresenting things and saying that Jesus was alive, the Pharisees would have produced the body and said, "Poppycock. Here he is. See, he's dead." But they didn't do that.

Yet another theory says that the women went to the wrong tomb. But others went to the tomb to verify their findings. And Joseph of Arimathea, who had donated his own tomb for Jesus, would certainly have corrected any such misunderstanding. You can be sure the Pharisees would have found the right tomb if it were as simple as that.

The way his followers treated his grave site is also evidence of the resurrection. When famous people die, everyone wants to go visit the grave. But Jesus' friends weren't bringing flowers to his grave site to pay their respects. They weren't hanging around the grave site because they knew he wasn't there.

The actions and testimony of all of Jesus' followers agree. The tomb was empty.

Why do you suppose Matthew included the account in 27:62-66?

Looking at the details of the resurrection, what stands out to you as significant?

What about the guards' report in 28:11-15 sounds similar to reasons for rejecting the resurrection today? How do you suppose the early disciples answered that accusation? Have you ever had to defend the validity of the resurrection? How did you do it?

Teaching Point Three: The witnesses of the resurrection are reliable.

Read 1 Corinthians 15:12-20.

The apostle Paul (when he was still called Saul) was the great antagonist of Christianity. Paul hated Jesus. He hated Christians and actively persecuted them. What could have turned him around other than the fact—as he writes to the Corinthian church—that he had met Jesus alive? He said he was as one born out of due time, one not even fit to be called a follower of Christ, because he himself had persecuted the church. This is evidence you can take seriously.

Paul, committed to the destruction of the Christian church, met Jesus and was dramatically changed. So when Paul arrived in Damascus, there were the Jewish rulers waiting to greet their hero and persecute the Christians. But Paul now believed in Jesus as the Messiah. The rulers must have been annoyed to learn that their champion of stifling this Christian "mythology" was now claiming that Jesus was alive.

Paul's original opposition to Christianity had been graphically illustrated when he gave approval of the stoning of the first Christian martyr, Stephen (Acts 7:59–8:1). A short time later when Paul testified that he had seen Jesus alive, you would think that others who were persecuting Christians would stop in their tracks and say, "If Saul of Tarsus thinks Jesus is alive, maybe we had better reevaluate our own position." But instead they were so antagonized that they took a vow not to eat or drink until they put Paul to death. In spite of that, Paul stuck to his story—through much personal persecution and even until his death.

Besides Paul's transformation, there were the remarkable transformations of Jesus' original apostles. Before Jesus' resurrection, they hid in fear and trembling. Peter was so frightened at the time of Jesus' trial that he denied even knowing Jesus. Only John and the women were mentioned as being at the cross when Jesus died. Yet after the resurrection, these same disciples devoted the rest of their lives to Jesus. And according to tradition—most of them even gave their lives for Jesus. Scripture tells us that James (the brother of John) was "put to death with the sword" on orders of King Herod (Acts 12:1, 2). The fearful Peter became a bold witness. Tradition says he was crucified upside down. Several of the others were said to have been crucified as well. Matthias was stoned and beheaded . . .

Finally, there were the difficult people who became convinced of Jesus' resurrection. The most difficult people to convince of anything are your family members. James, the brother of Jesus, having previously not believed in Jesus, became the leader of the church in Jerusalem. He had come to believe that his brother was alive.

And there are the five hundred people that Paul mentions in 1 Corinthians. You sometimes hear it said that Jesus' followers were so bereft that they hallucinated he'd come back from the grave. Go ask your favorite psychiatrist whether there is such a thing as mass hallucination. A real, live Jesus—not a hallucination—appeared to five hundred people at once.

In view of all this evidence, why do you suppose some of the Corinthians were saying that there was no resurrection of the dead?

Why would our faith be useless if there is no resurrection of the dead (v. 14)? How does the resurrection give you hope, both for this life and for the one to come?

 APPLY

The evidence is overwhelming: early accounts plus empty tomb plus eyewitness testimony equals the certainty that Jesus Christ was indeed resurrected from the dead as the ultimate authentication of his claim as the unique Son of God.

Look at all other religious leaders. Confucius, Buddha, and Mohammed are all in the grave. But Jesus Christ's tomb is empty. Jesus Christ alone possessed the power to overcome the grave.

The evidence points convincingly to Jesus Christ having told the truth when he said in John 11:25, "I am the resurrection and the life. He who believes in me will live, even though he dies."

Choose one of the following application options to do on your own this week. Turn to a partner and share your choice.

TRUST IN THE POWER

The power that raised Christ from the dead is available to you. Realizing this, are you dealing with a problem or situation that you have considered overwhelming or impossible? How can you rethink that and trust the Lord with it now? How can resting in that power change your perspective? Spend time meditating on 1 Corinthians 15 and share your findings with someone.

REVENGE OR FORGIVENESS?

In the article "Zacchaeus," Earl Palmer notes: "Have you ever noticed that after his resurrection, Jesus didn't come back to Pilate or Caiaphas and defeat them? Caiaphas went right on as high priest for another seven or eight years. Pilate went right on as procurator. Life went on as usual in a way. However, what Jesus did defeat were the weapons they had: death and fear" (p. 86).

Think through what you've studied today about Jesus' actions following his resurrection. If you had a second chance to get revenge—as Jesus did with Pilate and Caiaphas—would you take it? Or would you be able to let it go? Even with his *resurrection,* Jesus is teaching us how to live. Make an acrostic of F-O-R-G-I-V-E, filling it in with some practical ways you can forgive others who have wronged you. For example, the *F* might stand for "Find a positive result even from that bad experience." How can you also claim God's promises in those situations?

PERSONAL SUNRISE SERVICE

It doesn't have to be Easter or even a Sunday. You can celebrate Jesus' resurrection at any time. If you have a free morning, find a quiet place at a park, a favorite spot by a lake, or a grand view of a mountain. Take the elements of Communion and focus on what Jesus said they represent (Matthew 26:17-30). Read John 20, 21 in the *New Living Translation* or other contemporary version of Scripture. Spend time in prayer, thanking God for what his resurrection means to you. No free morning? Simply watch the sunrise from the driver's seat of your car on the way to work. Make it a time of remembrance by listening to worship music on a CD or MP3 player.

PRAY

Many churches have an Easter tradition of ringing bells, waving banners, and shouting in praise as they celebrate Jesus' resurrection. As a group, take time now to have your own celebration. Ring bells! Wave banners or colored paper! Shout it out: "He is risen!" End your celebration with "popcorn prayers" of praise—group members can spontaneously speak short prayers as they thank God for Jesus' resurrection and our own ultimate victory.

BEFORE NEXT TIME: *The leader should do an Internet search for several stories about a person (or pet) returning after a long absence: adopted people finding their birth parents, siblings separated for many years, people or pets lost in the wilderness for a period of time before they were found, or someone who was thought to be dead and then restored to life. Use search words such as* long lost, reunited, separated, *or* return, *along with the word* story, *and you should be able to quickly find a few of these accounts. Bring printouts of the stories to the next study.*

Promised Return | 6

The promise of Jesus' return should cause us
to live with a sense of urgency and hope.

*Much controversy, confusion, and mystery surround the topic of Jesus'
eventual return and the gathering of those who believe in him. One
thing is certain: Jesus said he would come back. And he promises eternal
life with him in Heaven to everyone who claims him as Lord.*

According to R. A. Torrey in his book Jesus Is Coming for You,
*the New Testament contains 318 references to Jesus' return. Obviously,
this event is very important for Christians and non-Christians alike.*

*In this study we'll look at Jesus' promise to return to earth, as well
as the life the Bible tells us we're offered if we follow him. We'll also
consider ways to live purposefully while we anticipate his coming.*

ΤΟΥΚΛΙΕΞΕΛΘΩΝΕΚΕΙΘΕΝΦΛΟΝΕ

BIBLE BASIS: *Matthew 16:24-27; 24:23-31; Mark 13:32-37; John 6:35-54; 10:18; 12:23-26; 14:1-4; 1 Thessalonians 4:13–5:11; 1 Peter 4:13*

EXTRA SUPPLIES: *printouts from the Internet of a few stories describing returns after a long absence*

 # LAUNCH

A group member who is willing can share a personal story of a special person (or pet) who was lost or taken away and then returned. Perhaps a teenager ran away for the weekend without calling, a child was lost in the mall for a few hours, or someone was reunited with a high school friend after many years. Allow a few minutes for the story to be told, including an emphasis on the feelings experienced. Then read or summarize a couple of the stories found online. Afterward, discuss the following:

Think of at least six emotions or feelings these people might have experienced when someone important to them returned after a long absence.

How are the stories we've just heard similar to Jesus' leaving earth for a time and then coming back in the future? How are they different? What emotions do you feel when you think about Jesus' return?

ΙΗϮΑΝΤΟΔΙΕϹШᵒ˟ΠΟϷΕΥΟΜΕΝΟΝ

 EXPLORE

Teaching Point One: Jesus promised to come back and to give eternal life to all his followers.

Read John 14:1-4.

As the disciples listened to Jesus say that he'd be leaving them, it struck terror in their hearts. How could they possibly go on living without him? Knowing that the disciples were afraid, Jesus comforted them with both his words and his promises.

What are your initial reactions to these verses? What comes to mind as you read Jesus' promise? When you picture Jesus preparing a place for you, what do you imagine?

Because Jesus is God, he could have "prepared a place for us" instantaneously. Why do you think he's chosen to wait a long time to return for us?

What do you think the disciples felt after hearing Jesus say these things? How do you feel after reading them?

Read John 6:35-54.

Jesus called himself "the bread of life" (v. 35). Our lives wouldn't last very long without bread (food). But when Jesus referred to "life," he was talking about more than just our physical existence. He was talking about a loving relationship with the living God who created us. Apart from Jesus, we can't experience this kind of life or relationship.

When you read that we are to eat Jesus' flesh and drink his blood, what do you think? What is the significance of Jesus' words?

What promises does Jesus make in these verses? What does Jesus say will happen to us when he returns? What is our responsibility?

Teaching Point Two: We don't know when it's going to happen, but we'll know it when it does!

Read Mark 13:32-37.

We find it hard to wait for anything. If we have to wait more than a few minutes in the checkout line at the grocery store, most of us roll our eyes at the slowness of the cashier and consider complaining to the store manager. So waiting for Christ to return is tough. Yet Jesus says that we should be on guard and alert as we watch for his return.

How can we wait with anticipation for Christ's kingdom to come? What do you think it means to "watch"?

How do these verses give you a sense of urgency and purpose in the way you live?

Read Matthew 24:23-31.

Jesus assured us that when he returns there won't be any doubt about it! Just as you can see a storm approaching from miles away, the moment of his return will be so full of glory and power that it won't be hidden from anyone.

What do you think the descriptive language in verses 27-29 means? Do you think these are literal descriptions of what Jesus' return will be like? When you think of Jesus' return, what do you picture?

What emotions do those mental pictures create in you? Do they make you afraid of Jesus' return, comforted by the images, or some other response? Explain.

What questions do these verses raise for you?

Teaching Point Three: We should live with Jesus' return always in mind.

Read 1 Thessalonians 4:13–5:11.

The Thessalonian Christians believed that Christ would return in their lifetime. But some believers began to pass away, and those left behind wondered how to resolve the deaths of their fellow Christians and the second coming of Christ. To answer their questions, Paul reminded them of God's sovereignty in history and his plan for Christ's return.

What do Jesus' death, resurrection, and return mean for those who believe in him? How can this passage comfort us when believers die?

Paul also exhorted the Thessalonian Christians to live with Jesus' return in mind: "But you, brothers, are not in darkness so that this day should surprise you like a thief. You are all sons of the light and sons of the day. We do not belong to the night or to the darkness. So then, let us not be like others, who are asleep, but let us be alert and self-controlled" (vv. 4-6). How will being alert and self-controlled prepare us for Jesus' return? What should that look like in your life?

Read Matthew 16:24-27.

How can we lose our lives for Christ's sake? By sharing in Jesus' sufferings. When we obey and serve God, we will inevitably face trials or troubles, which can make us feel like we're losing or missing out on a part of life. Yet that's precisely how we gain life in Christ. As Peter later wrote: "Rejoice that you participate in the sufferings of Christ, so that you may be overjoyed when his glory is revealed" (1 Peter 4:13).

In Daniel Meyer's "Come Die with Me," read the paragraph that begins at the top of page 88 with the words "I can't think." What might Jesus mean when he tells us to take up our crosses—to die with him?

Why is "losing your life" an important part of being prepared for Jesus' return? How does this play out in your life, practically speaking?

 APPLY

In the article "Come Die with Me," read the two paragraphs that begin with the words "A bridge to" at the bottom of page 91.

The promised return of Jesus is the final event in the process of our salvation. His return will be, in part, to bring us into the eternal life that he's offered. But we don't inherit this gift passively; we must take action ourselves to receive it. We must give up ourselves to take hold of Jesus.

While Christians have hope for the future because of Jesus' promised return, those who don't know him face a very uncertain future. We don't know when Jesus will come back; it could be hundreds of years from now—or it could be tomorrow. Knowing that, how should we live out our faith today?

Choose one of the following application options to do this week. Turn to a partner and share your choice.

BUCKET LIST

Some people have what they call a bucket list—things they want to do before they kick the bucket. Instead of making the usual bucket list, spend some time this week making a bucket list with a twist—things you think Jesus would want you to do before he returns. This could include things such as sharing the gospel with a specific person or changing something about the way you live.

DIE TO YOURSELF

Spend time in prayer this week, asking God what he wants you to die to. Be prepared for him to show you something unexpected that will be difficult for you to give up. Also ask him for the courage and strength to die to that thing for him.

BUILD A BRIDGE

Meyer says, "A bridge to new life stands at the place where someone once made some deliberate choices." You can be that bridge between death and new life for someone else. Make a list of three people you know who are not believers. Below their names, write some ideas for how you can be a bridge to God for them, and then commit to doing those things in the coming weeks.

 PRAY

The leader should pray aloud something similar to the following prayer. When the leader pauses, members can spend time in silent prayer, focusing on specifics that come to mind as a result of the leader's words.

"Lord, we thank you that you have promised to come back for us, and we know you'll be true to your word. Help us to live as if your return is imminent, because it may be. We know you are nudging us to stop doing certain things or start doing certain things. Give us strength and courage to respond." (pause)

"Lord, show us opportunities to tell family members, friends, coworkers, and neighbors about you, so the people we know and love can join in the anticipation of your return and receive the gift of eternal life that you offer to them." (pause)

"Finally, Lord, we thank you for the relationship we have with you now. We recognize and thank you for your love, your care, and your guidance." (pause)

"Amen."

BEFORE NEXT TIME: *Because this is the final study session in Crash Course on Jesus, the group might want to meet once more for fellowship and food and to spend time together celebrating the completion of this course. Members could scan the six sessions in this book before the get-together in order to find the most meaningful or life-changing thing they've gained from your study together. Then close the celebration with group members sharing that personal point. In addition, if your group plans to continue studying together, consider what Bible subject you want to tackle next. If you like the approach of this Crash Course study, check out www.standardpub.com for other titles in the series.*

FOR FURTHER RESEARCH

Note: The Crash Course series is designed to help you study important topics easily. The following magazine articles and books present additional valuable research. Items in the resource list are provided as a starting point for digging even deeper. Not everything in "For Further Research" is necessarily written from a conservative evangelical viewpoint. Great discussion and real learning happen when a variety of perspectives are examined in light of Scripture. We recommend that you keep a concordance and Bible dictionary nearby to enable you to quickly find Bible answers to any questions.

RESOURCE LIST

The Life and Ministry of Jesus: the Gospels (New Testament, Volume One in the Standard Reference Library, Standard Publishing, 2007). A through-the-Bible commentary that takes the reader from the manger to the empty tomb. Carefully weaving the details from all four Gospels into a single thread, the book gives a wonderful sense of the story of Jesus' life.

The Life & Teachings of Jesus (Holman Reference, 2008). Part of the Illustrated Bible Summary Series, this book draws on the four Gospels to provide an accessible and concise summary of Jesus' life and teachings.

More Than a Carpenter, Josh McDowell (Living Books, Tyndale, 1977, 2004). The quick-read classic, in which McDowell shares the evidence he found on his journey from agnostic to believer in Jesus.

Live Intimately: Lessons from the Upper Room, Lenya Heitzig and Penny Rose (David C. Cook, 2008). Featuring penetrating questions and life-changing applications, this user-friendly study examines Jesus' last night with his disciples before the crucifixion.

Jesus: A Novel, Walter Wangerin Jr. (Zondervan, 2005). This moving book explores the life of Jesus by imagining the thoughts, struggles, and joys of his mother, Mary, and his disciple John.

Jesus Mean and Wild: The Unexpected Love of an Untamable God, Mark Galli (Baker Books, 2008). This book explores passages in the Gospel of Mark that reveal an untamable and militant Messiah, providing a bold wake-up call for believers and a training manual for devoted disciples.

Jesus: The Greatest Life of All, Charles Swindoll (Thomas Nelson, 2008). Diving into the life of the Savior and taking his claims at face value, Swindoll's warmth and insight provide practical life application drawn straight from the words and works of Jesus.

Why Jesus Died, Gerard Sloyan (Augsburg Fortress, 2004). Although thousands of others died in the same way, the crucifixion of Jesus is uniquely remembered. Sloyan explores how Christ died, who was responsible, how his death came to be seen as redemptive, and how the event affected anti-Jewish sentiment.

Who Moved the Stone? Frank Morison (Zondervan, 1987). A classic apologetic on the subject of Jesus' resurrection. Morison began as a skeptic trying to prove the resurrection was a myth.

The Resurrection of the Son of God, N. T. Wright (Augsburg Fortress, 2003). Wright explores the very beginning of Christianity, starting with precisely what happened at Easter, including what the early Christians meant when they said that Jesus of Nazareth had been raised from the dead.

Jesus Is Coming for You, R. A. Torrey (Whitaker House Publishers, 1997). This book addresses some of the questions we have about Christ's return.

Your Eternal Reward: Triumph and Tears at the Judgment Seat of Christ, Erwin W. Lutzer (Moody Publishers, 1998). Learn more about what Jesus will be looking for in your life when he claims you into Heaven.

Christ's Birth and Your Birth

Christ's physical birth points to our need for a spiritual birth.

by John W. Yates II

On the wall in my church study hangs a precious photograph taken in a hospital room a couple of years ago. In this picture of a young couple from this church, a proud new dad still wears the surgical suit required in delivery rooms, as the brave new mom sits up in bed.

Clearly, both exhausted, there remains a joyous sparkle on their faces—expressions of peace, relief, pride, humility, and thankfulness all rolled together. In their arms, wrapped in white blankets, is a new-born son weighing 11 pounds and 1 ounce, measuring 23 inches long! At that moment, nothing in this world was more important than their baby. That's the way it is when a child is born.

At one moment in your life, you also were the most important person in the world to many people: your mother and father and family, who waited and prayed for nine long months. They celebrated and rejoiced that you'd come into the world.

Nothing can equal the birth of a child. Nothing should. A baby's birth is God's statement that the human race is worth continuing.

Recently, my mother told my children the story of the night I was born. On that night, my father and two older brothers unexpectedly had to transfer some horses, so they spent the night riding in the October moonlight for fifteen miles. My mom became restless and concerned as labor pains set in. The men were somewhere in the darkness on horseback, oblivious to the drama developing at home.

Most of us never tire of the story of the day or night when we were born—the big moment in our history when people laughed, cried, and hugged one another. They celebrated, perhaps even smoking cigars or drinking champagne. They forgot all their problems—at least for a while—just because of our birth.

Each Christmas, when we celebrate the birth of Jesus, we often hear another birth story that we never tire of hearing—even though we know the details by heart. While most people will soon forget the account of your birth or the story of how I was born, that's not true with Jesus' birth story. He's the Son of God.

JESUS' STORY

In many ways, Jesus' story is like yours and mine. Mary, his mother, endured the same discomfort and uncertainty about her unborn child that your mother did, and when he came, it was painful for him and for her. He was a helpless infant who needed to be sheltered, fed, clothed, and cleaned, just like all of us. But from the beginning, the very beginning, it was clear he was different from you and me. Joseph Cook says it so well in his carol "Gentle Mary Laid Her Child":

> Gentle Mary laid her Child, lowly in a manger;
> There he lay, the undefiled, to the world a Stranger; . . .
> Angels sang about His birth; wise men sought and found Him;
> Heaven's star shone brightly forth, glory all around Him;
> Shepherds saw the wondrous sight, heard the angels singing;
> All the plains were lit that night; all the hills were ringing. . . .
> Son of God, of humble birth, beautiful the story;
> Praise His name in all the earth, hail the King of glory!

God's own Son, born of a virgin—that claim is clear. The authors dare not have made up a tale about that most personal part of the story. Though Mary was his mother, and her body nurtured the seed that became the Son, Joseph was not the father. God, by a miracle of holy conception, put his very own seed into the womb of this maiden that had never slept with a man, and thereby God entered the human race. Jesus was wholly God and wholly man.

When Jesus was born, God came down from the heights of heaven in the person of Jesus. He wanted us to know what he's like at eye level. Jesus was born just as we were born. He lived and grew just as we did. However, at every stage, he showed us how to live. He lived a complete life, with no regrets and no sins. He lived this earthly life from a heavenly perspective. He saw as God in heaven sees and spoke as God in heaven speaks. And his words are the very words of God.

When we look at Jesus' life, we see so much in it that attracts us: his wisdom, power, consistency, insight, genius, strength, character, courage, sense of command, willingness to sacrifice, goodness, holiness, and wholeness.

Jesus is unique. Many great men and women have lived throughout history, but only one Jesus. No life has influenced the world as his. World leaders and famous people come and go. Their flames burn very brightly, but eventually their flames die down. Not so with Jesus. His flame still burns as brightly as ever because he still is. He still lives.

What's more, we need Jesus. Our lives are incomplete without him. And the message of his birth is that we can have him. Perhaps more accurately, he can have us. He's too mighty for us to have him.

How does it happen? How does the very Son of God become real in our lives?

OUR STORY

Before we can understand the present, we need to see how God was at work at the very beginning. In the first chapter of the Bible we find these words: "In the beginning God created the heavens and the earth. Now the earth was formless and empty, darkness was over the surface of the deep, and the Spirit of God was hovering over the waters" (Genesis 1:1, 2).

In the very beginning of everything we know, the Spirit of God was at work. God's Spirit brought about the creation of all things. Interestingly, the same word used for the work of the Holy Spirit in Creation is used by Luke in his gospel when he speaks of God's Spirit coming upon Mary. The angel told Mary that the Spirit of God would "overshadow" her (Luke 1:35), putting life in her—the life of Jesus, the life of God himself.

In the beginning, the Holy Spirit had put the same spiritual life into mankind. The presence of God was alive within man, woman, and child. That's what it means when the Bible says, "God created man in his own image, in the image of God he created him; male and female he created them" (Genesis 1:27). God was present in man's life. Man knew God, walking and talking with him. But man turned away from God, disobeying God and trampling upon the Spirit of God. So God withdrew his presence. God didn't take away his love or his concern, but the Spirit of God no longer dwelt within men and women. People were just people.

And people have made a mess of things, haven't they? While many brilliant and wonderful people have lived throughout history, we human beings have mostly wasted and squandered our God-given resources. We've made selfishness the most dominant and recurring theme in the world's history.

All of us are born sinful and selfish, grasping for ourselves and for our own. We see from our own perspective first and foremost. "Looking out for number one" is the most natural thing in the world. It's why we need laws, police, prisons, and armies: to preserve the peace and protect the vulnerable. We're all as different from Jesus as day is from night. He's the Son of God. We're just people.

A NEW STORY: CHRIST IN US

But that's not the end of God's story! The rest of the story is that the same Holy Spirit—who was present at creation and who came upon Mary to bring the Son of God to life as a human—is still present in the world. Because of this truth, we can know God ourselves.

I know that a lot of people say, "Certainly, I know God. I talk to God all the time. I believe in Jesus and God. I pray. I do good things all the time." But Jesus said that unless the same Holy Spirit who came upon Mary comes to live within you, you don't know God and you don't have God's life within you.

Let me give a simple analogy. A couple of summers ago, my two sons and I bought a lawn mower. My sons used this nice lawn mower to mow people's lawns in the summer and earn a little spending money. This mower is made to operate on a mixture of gasoline and oil. While it will run on just gasoline, if it doesn't have the oil, it's just a matter of time before it burns up. The oil enables the lawn mower to run as it's intended to run. The coming of the Spirit of God into your life is like putting oil in the machine. God created us in such a way that—if his Spirit is living inside us—we live life to the full. And we live forever—even beyond the grave.

However, without Christ in our life, we sputter. We never achieve our potential. And eventually, we break down altogether. We do the best we can. We eat, drink, work, play, and breathe. We take in information and process it all. Some of us even do all of this much better than others. But without the presence of God dwelling in our lives, it's like running the mower on gasoline alone and without the oil. Everything works for a while, and then it all breaks down. Many people, even in the church, live just this way. Perhaps you've been living this way yourself.

Jesus said that a change must take place in your life—a change every bit as dramatic and important as your own physical birth. In fact, he said it's like being born, except that instead of a physical birth, the birth he makes possible is spiritual.

Maybe this is what the poet Tennyson had in mind when, frustrated with himself, he cried out, "Oh, that a man might arise in me, that the man I am might cease to be!" (*Maud,* x. 5)

In a sense, that's what happens—although the person we are doesn't cease to be. Instead, the presence of the Lord Jesus comes into our lives and helps us become the persons God wants us to be. You see, there's a place inside each of us that was made for God. Either he comes to dwell there, or someone or something else dwells there. Only you and God know who dwells in that place in your life.

Many things might dwell in this place instead of God. It might be your family, your reputation, your career, a relationship with another person, pleasure, or knowledge. Many things can become God to us. But only when Christ becomes God to us—and when we give him the first place in our life—does the door open and allow the presence of God to come in and dwell in that place in our lives.

Even if you've done wonderful things, helped many people, prayed, gone to church, and worked tirelessly for good, it doesn't matter. Your life is incomplete and not running right until you beg God's forgiveness for putting any other thing before him, and until you decide that you want to be God's man or woman—God's son or daughter—and ask him to take over all of your life.

When you ask Christ to be at the center of your life, a celebration takes place in heaven even more wonderful than the celebration that took place in your family when you were physically born. Jesus told his friends that all the angels in heaven have a party when one single person turns from his own way and gives himself to God (see Luke 15:1-10). The same angelic host that rejoiced at the Bethlehem birth of Jesus rejoices when you ask Jesus to fill your life with his presence and make you his person.

IT'S TIME!

When you were born, you and your mother did a wonderful thing. Through her body, she let you know that it was time to be born. And you, tiny little person that you were, said, "Okay," and you were born!

God works in the same way with spiritual birth. He lets you know when it's time. He says, "Come to me. Let me take away those things in your life that should not be there: the pride that is unwilling to say, 'God, you have your way, I'm number two'; that unwillingness to forgive; that desire to be right; the need to be number one; the relationship that isn't the way it should be with mixed-up priorities; that temper; that jealousy; that lust."

God says, "Let me take these things away and bring into your life the Spirit of Christ. Believe in me, confess these things, and then let me wash them away and fill you with my presence. I will never leave you. As you follow me and trust me and obey me, I will begin to make you whole. And what I begin to do in your life now, I'll complete in you throughout eternity."

Right at this moment, think about yourself and your God. Think about turning your life over to him. Allow him to fill your life with his very presence. It's the most important thing you can ever do.

Being born is such a simple process. We simply cooperate with our mother. Spiritual birth is equally simple. We simply cooperate with our heavenly Father. He says to us, "This is the time to let me come into your life and take control."

Then we say, "Yes. Yes, Lord, I believe, and I give all of myself that I can to all that I know of you."

Zacchaeus

Jesus came to conquer evil, but not in the way the Jews expected.

by Earl Palmer

Remember the account of Zacchaeus, the short-of-stature tax collector? I've always had a soft spot for this man, because he was short, and I'm not so tall either.

Here's the way Luke began this story in his gospel: "[Jesus] entered Jericho and was passing through. And there was a man named Zacchaeus; he was a chief tax collector, and rich" (Luke 19:1, 2, *RSV*). That's a loaded phrase—because apparently, the little man was loaded.

"And he sought to see who Jesus was, but could not, on account of the crowd, because he was small of stature. So he ran on ahead and climbed up into a sycamore tree to see him, for he was to pass that way" (vv. 3, 4, *RSV*).

Notice that Zacchaeus was a smart man. He figured which way Christ was going and then Zacchaeus went on ahead and got up in that tree.

Maybe he even said to himself, "Maybe Jesus will stop nearby and argue with the Pharisees. I understand he's always arguing with Pharisees, and maybe a group of those laymen down from Jerusalem will argue with him. And maybe I could get it all on my recorder and take it to the tax collector meeting." Think of all the things that might have gone through Zacchaeus' mind as he saw Jesus coming.

Luke specified that Zacchaeus climbed into a sycamore tree. Unlike an olive tree—which has tiny leaves—the sycamore tree is full and leafy. Zacchaeus could sit in this tree and see Jesus if he came, but at the same time be pretty well hidden.

As I said, I've always had a soft spot for Zacchaeus. He's a man after my heart. One thing about short people is they tend to think ahead. I remember that Nehru came to UC-Berkeley when I was an undergraduate. I was taking a course on the politics of Pakistan and India, and I was excited to see him. I saw a huge limousine outside the Greek Theater with some Secret Service men around it, and like Zacchaeus, I figured, that must be where he's going after he speaks. And so, the moment the event was over, while people were still applauding, I ran down to get next to that limousine so that I could see Nehru up close. It worked. I stood just a few yards from Nehru as he walked by.

JESUS RESTORED ZACCHAEUS

Of course, from his perch in the sycamore tree, Zacchaeus got a little more than he bargained for. "When Jesus came to the place, he looked up and said to him, 'Zacchaeus, make haste and come down; for I must stay at your house today.' So he made haste and came down, and received him joyfully. And when they saw it, they all murmured, 'He has gone in to be the guest of a man who is a sinner'" (vv. 5-7, RSV).

"They all murmured." I think this is the only place in the New Testament where everyone in the crowd reacted the same way. We read in some places that scribes and Pharisees murmured or that the Sadducees murmured. But here, "They all murmured." The scribes, Pharisees, Herodians, zealots, disciples—everyone was murmuring: "He has gone in to be the guest of a man who is a sinner."

We must appreciate the vicious institution that tax collecting was in the first century. The Romans used the same practice as the Persians when they conquered. They didn't take the conquered people back to Rome and show them off as hostages, because then they'd have to feed all those prisoners. They learned not to take prisoners, but to set up defeated nations in their own economies and then tax them. But in order to tax people, especially when they didn't have bank accounts, the tax collectors needed people on the inside who knew where the wealth was. So they got collaborators. They found a man like Zacchaeus and elevated him to become a chief tax collector. They protected these people with Roman garrisons so no one dared tamper with them, and yet gave these citizens the right to point out where the wealth was. They said to the Roman officials, "Now that person has 90 sheep up in Bethlehem. I've known this family for years. You'd never know it to look at his house, but that man's loaded." So the Romans could tax him all the more.

Notice how the tax collector got it both ways. Of course, to some extent they deserved what they got, because there was corruption in the institution. People would come up to a tax collector and say, "Hey, don't tell them I've got 90 sheep up in Bethlehem. It will ruin me."

So the tax collector would say, "Okay, I won't tell them. But what do I get for it?" Then a little bribe would pass under the table. But then the tax collector would tell the Romans anyway. The citizens despised the institution because tax collectors used a privileged relationship to exploit their own people.

Next, Luke records: "Zacchaeus stood and said to the Lord, 'Behold, Lord, the half of my goods I give to the poor; and if I have defrauded any one of anything, I restore it fourfold'" (v. 8, *RSV*). I don't know what happened between Zacchaeus and Jesus Christ, but this was a man who repented immediately and in a concrete way! He didn't say a lot of drivel about how sorry he was. He just said, "Fourfold I will restore to those I've defrauded" (this was a nice way of admitting that he had done something wrong), "and half of my goods I give to the poor."

Repentance in the biblical sense (*metanoia*) means to turn around, and—whether or not you say you're sorry—change and do something. You head a different direction. That's what Zacchaeus did here.

Then Jesus spoke to Zacchaeus, and these last two sentences are incredible sentences: "And Jesus said to him, 'Today salvation has come to this house'" (v. 9, *RSV*). Salvation is the Greek word *soteria*. In the Septuagint, it's one of the words used to translate the Hebrew word *shalom*. This word salvation expresses the peace of the Old Testament, meaning health, restoration, and wholeness. So when Jesus says, "salvation has come," he means "shalom has come—salvation has come—to this house, since he also is a son of Abraham."

Notice that Jesus then restored Zacchaeus as a son of Abraham. The very thing that Zacchaeus had thrown away in his profession was the dignity of being a Jew. At the expense of his own people, he exploited his nationality for the benefit of the Romans. But Jesus restored his sonship in front of everyone. The last sentence is important: "For the Son of man came to seek and to save the lost" (v. 10, *RSV*).

This whole event includes a series of surprises, and I want to reflect on four of them.

The first surprise is that Jesus noticed one person in a great crowd. We don't expect that from famous people. If you've ever met a famous person, you don't expect that person to take time to talk to you. If you've ever been in a line where you have had a chance to shake the hand of the President of the United States, protocol people stand right next to the President, get your name, and say your name to the President. Then, while he's shaking your hand, he's looking to the next person. That's how they move the line along. You'd be rather surprised if he stopped and said, "How's it going in your church? How's that problem with the carpet?" Yet Jesus, throughout his entire ministry, gave everyone his full attention. It's one of the marks of Christ's ministry.

You see it here. Jesus was sensitive to everybody he met. You never get the feeling in the New Testament that Jesus was talking to someone and juggling oranges at the same time. He gave that person his full attention.

The second surprise is that Jesus accepted the hospitality of a person so hated by the people (and for good cause).

The third surprise was that a man like Zacchaeus, who made his whole fortune by being hardhearted, became so repentant and generous.

The final surprise is that a man who did so much real harm in his life should be restored publicly by Jesus as a son of Abraham.

All of these surprises come together in one interesting and intense sentence: "They all murmured, 'He has gone in to be the guest of a man who is a sinner.'" If you can understand why the crowd was so upset, then you'll be able to understand the very heart of the gospel of Jesus Christ.

The people were upset because they expected a Messiah who would conquer evil. Many of them were hoping that Jesus would be that Messiah. Make no mistake, our Lord was famous at this point. He was in the very territory where John the Baptist had said so many things about him. Even Zacchaeus was so impressed by the faith of Jesus that he'd gone ahead of the great crowds and climbed up a tree to make sure he could see Jesus. The people were expecting the Messiah—but they were seeking a political savior who would conquer the evil of the oppressive Roman empire. Jesus disappointed that expectation.

I've often said one of the most elegant and most incredible proofs of our Lord's messiahship is how wonderfully he both fulfills and disappoints every expectation we have.

Take a look at Luke 3. Luke was very interested in John the Baptist, and he provided a long narration of John the Baptist's speeches. The people were "in expectation, and all men questioned in their hearts concerning John, whether perhaps he were the Christ" (Luke 3:15, *RSV*). Think about how famous John the Baptist was. Did you know in some ways he was more famous in many parts of the Holy Land than Jesus was? Even after Jesus' resurrection, followers of John the Baptist still worked in North Africa. In fact, one of them was Apollos, who came up to Corinth and had never heard about Christ. He was still looking for the Messiah. He was a follower of John the Baptist. Because of his fame and even some of his rhetoric, some people wondered if John was the Messiah.

"John answered them all, 'I baptize you with water; but he who is mightier than I is coming, the thong of whose sandals I am not worthy to untie.'" That one line appears in all four gospels and also the Book of Acts. "'He will baptize you with the Holy Spirit and with fire'" (v. 16, *RSV*). (By the way, John didn't mean fire to warm your heart; he meant fire to burn up the evildoers.) "His winnowing fork [a huge fork used to clear and to slice away] is in his hand, to clear his threshing floor, and to gather the wheat into his granary [that will be the good people, the sons of righteousness and God's beloved], but the chaff he will burn with unquenchable fire" (v. 17, *RSV*). That's what John the Baptist expected of the Messiah.

As you know, a few days after John spoke these words, Jesus appeared and John said, "Behold, the Lamb of God, who takes away the sin of the world!" (John 1:29, *RSV*). In his commentary on John's gospel, Raymond Brown says it's probably not correct for us to think when John spoke these words that he was thinking of Isaiah 53, the suffering servant lamb, because all Jews by the time of the first century thought of Isaiah 53 as referring to Israel, not to the Messiah. The Messiah would be the ensign who would startle the nations.

Look at Malachi 3, 4, which provides a great clue to John the Baptist's preaching. Note where chapter 3 starts: "Behold, I send my messenger to prepare the way before me" (Malachi 3:1, *RSV*). And then chapter 4: "'For behold, the day comes, burning like an oven, when all the arrogant and all evildoers will be stubble; the day that comes shall burn them up,' says the LORD of hosts, 'so that it will leave them neither root nor branch'" (Malachi 4:1, *RSV*). Notice how similar this is to what John the Baptist spoke. "'But for you who fear my name the sun of righteousness shall rise, with healing in its wings. You shall go forth leaping like calves from the stall. And you shall tread down the wicked, for they will be ashes under the soles of your feet, on the day when I act,' says the LORD of hosts. . . . 'Behold, I will send you Elijah the prophet before the great and terrible day of the LORD comes'" (vv. 2, 3, 5, *RSV*).

So we realize now that the Jews were looking for a Messiah who would conquer evil. He would reach his hand into the horrible wheel of Roman injustice, take hold of that wheel, and right it. He would destroy the evildoers.

ZACCHAEUS GAINED GROUND, BUT JESUS LOST IT

When Jesus called Zacchaeus down from the tree and announced he was spending the night at Zacchaeus' house, you can understand why everyone was shocked and "they all murmured." But look what Jesus did. He healed Zacchaeus. Notice he used the word salvation, the word for healing. Jesus saved Zacchaeus. And then he restored the identity of Zacchaeus.

As a result, Zacchaeus gained ground. I've been in ministry long enough to tell when the grace of God has gotten hold of somebody's life. Their hands loosen up. They become generous. They want to give half of their goods away. They want to restore all those they've defrauded. They don't just say they're sorry or play games. They do something, because Christ has come into their hearts. Zacchaeus gained ground. And then Luke writes that Zacchaeus "received [Jesus] joyfully" (Luke 19:6, *RSV*). Zacchaeus became generous and expansive.

However, Jesus lost ground. Make no mistake about it, the shadow of the Cross was over this event. . . . The people were expecting a Messiah who would conquer evil. They expected the defeat of evil. But no one in the first century expected that Jesus would defeat evil in the way he chose. Listen closely to the way Jesus chose to defeat evil. This passage provides an important clue: Jesus would defeat evil by taking it upon himself, by absorbing its anger, its power. Then he, himself, would disarm that power. And Jesus would defeat evil by identifying with the sinner. Notice, "the Son of man came to seek and to save the lost" (v. 10, *RSV*). He identified with you and me, and then he went to the Cross for us.

Notice, too, that Jesus found Zacchaeus. And this was surprising, because instead of blasting this sinner, Jesus Christ knew he would die and take Zacchaeus' place. He showed that he would be the lamb of Isaiah 53. Jesus would conquer evil by absorbing it, by taking it to himself, by identifying with the sinners. "For our sake he made him to be sin who knew no sin, so that in him we might become the righteousness of God" (2 Corinthians 5:21, *RSV*).

Jesus never intended to be the Messiah who would defeat evil with brute force. He knew he would conquer evil with his own sacrifice. Have you ever noticed that after his resurrection, Jesus didn't come back to Pilate or Caiaphas and defeat them? Caiaphas went right on as high priest for another seven or eight years. Pilate went right on as procurator. Life went on as usual in a way. However, what Jesus did defeat were the weapons they had: death and fear.

He conquered those and the power of the Devil. Jesus Christ fulfilled Elijah's prophecy. He fulfilled John the Baptist's prophecy, but in a way that no one expected. He identified with Zacchaeus, and now Zacchaeus gained ground because of that identification.

That's the love of God! This isn't a parable or a sermon illustration about love. It's the very existence of love itself. And we have love that comes alongside us in many ways—love that's an event, love that's powerful and able to give new life, a love that totally surprises all of our expectations. Even Jesus' own disciples were totally surprised by what Jesus does.

Love was Jesus spending the night with Zacchaeus—identifying with the repentant tax collector and absorbing in himself all the tragedy of Zacchaeus' life. That was how he set Zacchaeus free.

Jesus offers the same to us—he's willing to absorb all the tragedy and trials of our lives in order to set us free.

© Earl Palmer. Used with permission. This article was adapted from a sermon by Earl Palmer, and originally published on Preaching Today Audio or PreachingToday.com, resources of Christianity Today International.

Come Die with Me

When Jesus really scares me

by Daniel Meyer

Matthew's gospel says that toward the end of his three years of public ministry, "Jesus began to explain to his disciples that he must go to Jerusalem and suffer many things at the hands of the elders, chief priests and teachers of the law, and that he must be killed and on the third day be raised to life." Hearing this, "Peter took [Jesus] aside and began to rebuke him. 'Never, Lord!' he said. 'This shall never happen to you!'" (Matthew 16:21, 22).

What Jesus said next in the face of Peter's apparent devotion consistently forces me to define discipleship in terms I don't think I'd ever get to by myself. The Bible says that "Jesus turned and said to Peter, 'Get behind me, Satan! You are a stumbling block to me; you do not have in mind the things of God, but the things of men.' Then Jesus said to his disciples, 'If anyone would come after me, he must deny himself and take up his cross and follow me. For whoever wants to save his life will lose it, but whoever loses his life for me will find it'" (vv. 23-25).

I can't think of anything that Jesus ever spoke that seems scarier. This particularly holds true when you contrast these words with some of Jesus' other invitations. For example, when Jesus says, "Come dine with me"—come experience my fulfillment—most of us are pleased to accept. When Christ says, "Come do life with me"—experience the difference my companionship makes—many of us are naturally intrigued. When Jesus says, "Come dance with me"—come experience my joy—it seems like a good deal to follow him. But when Jesus says, "Come die with me"—come take up a cross with me, come experience my death—there is something in almost all of us that cries out with the apostle Peter, "Never, Lord!"

However, our "Never, Lord" often means something like "No thanks!" And that's only natural. Beginning with the cradle, we learn that the goal of life is to preserve it. From the moment we're first strapped into our child safety seats to the day we lie in a hospital room with tubes in our bodies, the continual message is: Preserve, protect, sustain, secure!

In addition, early in life we absorb the message that the quality of one's life is directly related to the quantity of the life-enhancements we can secure. We end up defining our lives by the titles and trophies we amass, the pleasures and privileges we enjoy, the sheepskins and the shape of our skin we achieve, the castles and coin-collections we create.

SOMEONE MUST DIE

Jesus comes along and reminds us that we define life too superficially, too selfishly, too stupidly. He looks right into our eyes and tells us that we barely touch life as God intended it. He tells us to get off the fence we've been on that straddles the world's way and the kingdom's way. He calls us to patrol the pleasures we've allowed to invade our perimeter and conquer our hearts. He tells us to check our bags for the anxiety, fear, and anger we've been carrying so long that we don't see how burdened and blocked we still are by it.

And, if we're going to follow Jesus through the gate of the kingdom—if we're to be born anew into this life of God—then the way we've been taught to define life, the way we've naturally come at life, the life or self we've become, has to die. It has to be lost. It has to be named and nailed and annihilated. And that will be painful and hard. It will demand something of the profound humility and courageous perseverance we see in Jesus as he carries his cross.

Dying in this way will mean periods of terrible thirsting for the substances that used to slake our thirst. It will mean times when we'll feel utterly forsaken by God. It will put us in a place of temporary vulnerability before the soldiers and mocking crowds of this world. It will mean cleaving to our spiritual family in the way Mary and John were called to by Christ at the cross. It will require our daily commitment into the Father's hands. It means a trusting obedience until God's work in and through us is completed here and we can say: "It is finished."

George MacDonald, the great Scottish preacher, once wrote: "Christ died to save us, not from suffering, but from ourselves; not from injustice, far less from justice, but from being unjust. He died that we might live—but live as He lives, by dying as He died who died to Himself that He might live unto God. If we do not die to ourselves, we cannot live to God, and he that does not live to God is dead."

We're accustomed to focusing on the death that the Palm Sunday crowd eventually called for. But if we stop there, we miss much of the meaning of Good Friday and the Easter beyond. It's equally crucial that we remember the death that Christ called for when he said, "If anyone would come after me, he must deny himself and take up his cross and follow me. For whoever wants to save his life will lose it, but whoever loses his life for me will find it" (Matthew 16:24, 25).

This death Christ calls for is a price entirely worth paying. It's the path to communion with God himself. It's the road to an eternal peace and prosperity. It's the only way to gain an unshakable faith, an unconquerable hope, and a life-changing love more precious than anything the crowds chase after. But this is what Jesus makes clear: This life doesn't come from simply wearing a cross; it comes from bearing a cross.

Somebody—some life, some self—has to die.

THE *DA VINCI CODE* JESUS

No wonder they crucified Jesus. No wonder even some of Jesus' would-be disciples said: "Never, Lord. I don't like this path you're talking about."

I understand that. I understand why people still want to crucify Christ instead of die to self. Sometimes, I wonder if I'd rather have Dan Brown's *Da Vinci Code* Jesus. I'd like to rewrite the story of Jesus and make him someone who'd never really insist on such difficult choices. Maybe it would be far easier to view Jesus as someone who'd never do something so radical as to deny himself the pleasure of sex, who'd give in and get married to Mary Magdalene and father a child, and whose real gospel was about touching the divine through physical pleasures and fertility.

If I can come to view the church of Jesus in the *Da Vinci Code* way—as just a collection of corrupt or misguided people—or if I can simply caricature spiritual disciplines as some sort of sick, twisted masochism, that would be freeing, in a way. How liberating to take just the parts of the biblical Jesus that I like—the ones that reinforce my lifestyle and leave me feeling spiritual without much cost. I can wear a cross as jewelry without feeling any need to bear a cross as a disciple. I can go on with life as I have it. I can keep the self I have.

But I don't want that self. I want a better self. How about you? Don't you want the self that Jesus shows you, that Jesus says can be born in you, the kind of self he apparently gave to Arland D. Williams, Jr.?

CROSS AT THE BRIDGE

Does the name Arland Williams mean anything to you? If you've ever spent time in the Washington D.C. area, you might know that a bridge by that name crosses the Potomac River. I wasn't far from there on January 13, 1982, when Air Florida Flight 90 iced up upon takeoff and crashed into the icy waters of the river moments later. I remember watching—as many people did on the news—the struggle to rescue the small number of survivors who treaded water for their life. Arland Williams was among the survivors.

As the *Washington Post* told it: "Five different times, a helicopter dropped a rope to save Williams. Five times, Williams passed the rope to other passengers in worse shape than he was. When the rope was extended to Williams the sixth time, he could not take hold, and succumbed to the frigid waters. His heroism was not rash. Aware that his own strength was fading, [Williams] deliberately handed hope to someone else." Again and again and again and again and again and again, in the most difficult circumstances, Arland Williams made the choice to die to self.

A bridge to new life stands at the place where someone once made some deliberate choices. "No one takes [my life] from me," Jesus said to Peter and the other disciples shortly before walking to the cross. "No one takes it from me, but I lay it down of my own accord" (John 10:18). Jesus said: "The hour has come for the Son of Man to be glorified. I tell you the truth, unless a kernel of wheat falls to the ground and dies, it remains only a single seed. But if it dies, it produces many seeds. The man who loves his life will lose it, while the man who hates his life in this world will keep it for eternal life. [For] whoever serves me must follow me" (John 12:23-26).

We need to remember that when he might have elected otherwise, Jesus chose to take up his cross and pay the ultimate price for human sin, so that we might be forgiven and live forever with God. Jesus chose to pass the rope of salvation to us. If you've never taken hold of it before, grab hold today. Let Christ pull you to safety, and wrap you in the blanket of his family.

But don't stop there. Don't let the cross merely be a symbol of the life Jesus had or that you'll have in heaven. Let it be a signpost to the life Christ calls you to in this world. Cross over the bridge and into the life of the kingdom of God. You know the way into that city, don't you? It's marked out by Jesus, by Arland, and by every soul in every home and church and workplace and town who keeps making the difficult choice—the disciple's choice:

"If [you] would come after me," said Jesus, "[you] must deny [your]self and take up [your] cross and follow me."

Sometimes, this call and cross causes us to tremble. But it's the tremble of new life.

© Daniel Meyer. Used with permission. This article was adapted from a sermon by Daniel Meyer, and originally published on Preaching Today Audio or PreachingToday.com, resources of Christianity Today International.

FIND SPIRITUAL FORMATION TOOLS at Christian BibleStudies.com

▶ Join over **125,000 people** who use ChristianBibleStudies.com

▶ Choose from **over 800 downloadable Bible studies** to find exactly what you're looking for

▶ Study through a book of the Bible **verse-by-verse**, discuss an important topic from Scripture, or learn about **hot topics** like movies and politics

▶ Pay only once and make up to **1,000 copies**

▶ Enhance your personal devotions, small groups, or Sunday School classes

▶ Facilitate **lively discussions** with fascinating topics

a service of

CHRISTIANITY TODAY
INTERNATIONAL

BUILD AN EFFECTIVE MINISTRY with Small Groups.com

Inspiring
Life-Changing
Community

▶ Learn how to **start or re-start** both small groups and entire ministries

▶ Choose from thousands of **training tools, Bible studies, and free articles** from trusted leaders like Philip Yancey, Les and Leslie Parrott, and Larry Crabb

▶ Connect your group with a free and fun **social-networking tool**

▶ **Train yourself and your leaders** with invaluable assessments and orientation guides

▶ Downloadable resources are ready for **immediate use** and can be copied up to 1,000 times

▶ Join the **blog conversation** and share your small-group experiences

a service of

CHRISTIANITY TODAY
INTERNATIONAL

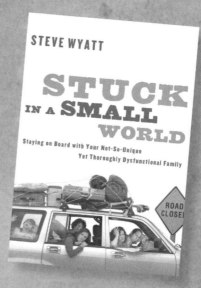
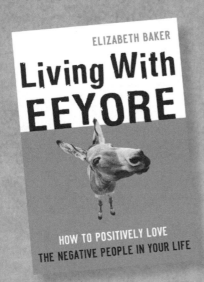